# Transcending Illness
## through the
# Power of Belief

Adolfo Quezada

iUniverse, Inc.
Bloomington

# Transcending Illness through the Power of Belief

iUniverse books may be ordered through booksellers or by contacting:

iUniverse
1663 Liberty Drive
Bloomington, IN 47403
www.iuniverse.com
1-800-Authors (1-800-288-4677)

ISBN: 978-1-4620-6971-2 (sc)
ISBN: 978-1-4620-6975-0 (e)

Printed in the United States of America

iUniverse rev. date: 11/30/2011

# Transcending Illness
## through the
# Power of Belief

# Other Books by Adolfo Quezada

*Loving Yourself for God's Sake*

*Heart Peace: Embracing Life's Adversities*

*Rising from the Ashes: A Month of
Prayer to Heal Our Wounds*

*Sabbath Moments: Finding Rest for the
Soul in the Midst of Daily Living*

*Compassionate Awareness: Living Life to the Fullest*

*Radical Love: Following the Way of Jesus*

*For Joni, Alicia, Sharon, Dorothy,
Alejandra, Ave, and Melanie*

# The Beatitudes of Illness

*Blessed are the poor in health, for theirs is the realm of holiness.*

*Blessed are those who mourn the loss of physical energy, for they will evoke the strength of their spirit.*

*Blessed are those who are humbled by illness, for they will be lifted up on the wings of their soul.*

*Blessed are those who hunger for deep healing and thirst for total wellness, for they will be filled with hope.*

*Blessed are those who forgive the betrayal of their mind and body, for they will bring union to their divided self.*

*Blessed are those whose heart is pure and true, for they will share the haleness of God.*

*Blessed are those who make peace with their infirmities, for they will be called healers of God.*

*Blessed are those whose well-being is persecuted by genetics, accidents, or other forces beyond their control, for they will discover purpose to their affliction.*

# Contents

# Foreword

have been blessed to know Adolfo Quezada for four decades. He has been a grace to me through all these years. I wish you too could know personally the author of this book.

But you will have a good look into Adolfo's soul as you read *Transcending Illness through the Power of Belief.* This book looks right into the eyes of two realities we do not like to think about: sickness and death. This book not only invites us to think about them, but also challenges us to embrace them in their reality and totality. Is this even possible?

At first glance we may say "no." But as we read these pages we discover that our embrace of illness and death actually becomes the source of an interior peace we may have not yet experienced in our lives.

I recommend *Transcending Illness through the Power of Belief* to anyone who may prefer not to think of these realities. And to anyone who thinks of them with considerable discomfort and fear. And to those of us who have experienced or are experiencing illness, or who have suffered from the death of a loved one or, perhaps, even glanced at one's own death. My cardiologist informed me recently that I had a serious condition that he could not treat without the implantation of a defibrillator and pacemaker. As I was experiencing this, *Transcending Illness through the Power of Belief* came into my hands.

These pages helped bring me to embrace—not just accept, but embrace—my body and illness for what it was. It helped me embrace the inevitability of death at some time with peace and even joy.

Adolfo is a gifted writer. God has blessed him with the ability to express in the right words his deepest thoughts and emotions. I thank God for Adolfo and for his book. I hope it will bring you to embrace life, death, and everything we encounter on this beautiful journey we are on.

Msgr. Robert D. Fuller

Author of *Adventures of a Collegial*

*Parish and Homilies from the Heart*

# Preface

*The human spirit will endure sickness; but a broken spirit—who can bear.* (Proverbs 18:14)

The title of this book, *Transcending Illness through the Power of Belief*, means much more than the restoration of what has been diseased or broken, and it is more than the "curing" of our physical illness. It means the return we make to our true nature as holy beings. In the context of this book, "holiness" does not refer to an official designation attributed through religious use or by ecclesiastical authority, but to our essential sacredness as human beings. Holiness or wholeness can describe a person's overall health even if that person has an illness or an injury. It refers to our total being, to our inclusive existence, and to our intrinsic value. Holiness refers to the inclusion of all our parts, be they light or dark, creative or destructive, feminine or masculine. When we embrace our total being, we promote healing from the soul.

Because what we believe to be real is what ultimately counts, the power of belief can affect our body, mind, and spirit positively or negatively. It can help to heal us or make us sick. Sometimes the power of our belief can actually create the symptoms of a disease that we don't really have, and, conversely, our belief can help to heal us of a disease that we do have. Because our body, mind, and spirit are interdependent and integrally connected, how we believe mentally affects how we feel physically and emotionally. Our mind passes on information to our body at the cellular level, so, if we believe in the power to heal ourselves, our body receives this information and responds accordingly.

When we believe in the divine energy that flows through us, we open up to that energy. When we believe in the natural laws on which life itself is based, we commit to living our lives in harmony with those laws. Our belief emanates from deep within the soul and beckons us toward healing and holiness. At our core is a divinely drafted blueprint for healing. But although there are commonalities among all of us, no two persons respond exactly the same way to the healing forces of nature. Our responsibility as self-healers is to discover what works for us personally and what doesn't, and then to honor and obey the wisdom of our unique blueprint.

Being diagnosed with a serious illness is shocking and unexpected to us; it turns our world upside down, leaving chaos and confusion, fear and anxiety in its wake. We plead desperately that this cup may pass us by, yet, when the dust begins to settle and we accept that we are indeed seriously ill, there is clarity that reveals insights into our life that we have never had before.

Serious illness strips us of our defenses and forces us to deal with whatever is ailing us at a deeper level. We may discover that what sickens us on the surface is but a sign that there is imbalance or disharmony within. Paradoxically, the same illness from which we suffer can reveal to us the antidote for what ails us and can become a powerful healing agent.

In the course of our illness we have the time, although not always the gumption, to reflect on our life and to delve into the deeper, spiritual place within our self. In this profound and sacred place we encounter the soul. The soul is the womb of life, the cradle of our being, and the crux of all healing.

If our illness is diagnosed as terminal, our life changes dramatically. At first, we are in shock and disbelief that this could be happening to us. Eventually, the reality of our mortality begins to sink in. The awareness of our inexorable death sentence compels us to live authentically. Knowing that we are going to die soon makes us impatient with anything that is not real. We don't have time to waste on fantasy or pretext. Awareness of our impending death evokes honesty and unpretentiousness. In fact, the closer death comes to us, the more genuine and humble we become. The imminence of our death also helps us to reset our priorities in life. In the light of death, that which is truly significant rises to the top of our attention, while the less significant drops to the bottom. Living in congruence with what matters most to us now brings us the accordance the soul requires.

# Introduction

Transcending Illness through the Power of Belief is purposely a small book because its message is clear and simple: we heal from the inside out. This is not a book about "faith healing" that claims that with enough faith all physical and mental ailments will be cured. Rather, its premise is that what we believe in our conscious or unconscious mind profoundly affects the state of our health positively or negatively. While we may take advantage of externals, such as medicine and medical treatments, to enhance our good health, it is what we believe about our self, our life, and our healers that influences the healing process most. The soul—that is, the core of who we are—uses anything, including illness, to heal the disharmony and imbalance within us that contribute to illness. A deep healing happens at the level of the soul that leads to holiness (wholeness).

For twenty-five years I have offered counseling and psychotherapy services to thousands of men and women suffering from the effects of trauma and/or chronic illnesses. During that time I have also conducted spiritual retreats and seminars on overcoming stress, anxiety, grief, and depression. In addition, I wrote a psycho-spiritual newspaper column, "Of Mind and Spirit," that helped many over the years. I am confident that the combination of these experiences has uniquely qualified me to write Transcending Illness through the Power of Belief. I am hopeful that what I have written will serve as inspiration and encouragement to those who must travel the path of serious illness.

# Transcending Our Illness

To transcend our illness we enter into it with our whole body, mind, and spirit. We experience all that it has to offer us, and we learn all that it has to teach us. We move beyond the illness and beyond the cure to holiness (wholeness), which is our true nature. Serious illness is a small death that robs us of that which has defined us. It forces us to see our self in the light of reality. Idealized images of our self drop away because we no longer have the energy to sustain them. Mired in the illness, we can no longer pretend to be who we are not, and who we want to be must change as well. Our illusion of self-sufficiency is shattered, and our attitude toward others changes radically. If before we had been helpers, we are now recipients of help. If before we had been too busy to stop and be with others, we are now ready to pause and be with them. Serious illness gives us the opportunity to slow down and, perhaps for the first time, be available to life. In fact, all we can do is hold on, breathe, wait, and be with what is. Like it or not, we are now restricted in such a way that we have no place to go but within. In this undistracted place deep within us, the necessary healing begins to take place.

Our illness is an opportunity for deep healing. When we are seriously ill or injured, it may be that we are being admonished by life to stop, listen, and learn. The symptoms that announce our illness are not the enemy, but the herald that forewarns us that serious consequences may be coming. We ignore, discount, or medicate away the symptoms at our own peril. If, on the other hand, we heed the symptoms and respectfully learn from them what is happening to us and why, we move toward healing.

Our illness may be the consequence of many years of self-neglect, bad diet, lack of exercise, overwork, or unresolved personal and family problems. It would be wrong, however, to assume that all illness is our fault or that it is always contingent on self-care or good behavior. Sometimes we get seriously ill even if we have taken very good care of our self and have lived uprightly. Illness can come from external sources to which we become vulnerable. These include genetics, the environment, epidemics, war, accidents, toxins, viruses, bacteria, and others. Whether from natural or unnatural causes, illness is a part of life in this world. Just as the wheat and the weeds grow in the field together, health and illness are a polarity with which we must contend.

Serious illness is the ultimate poverty, the great loss, the supreme humiliation, the grave deprivation, the merciless state, the bare heart. Exposed and vulnerable, we have no choice but to allow the illness of our body to be what it is. In other words, we surrender. But our surrender is not resignation; instead, it is acceptance of our present reality. The word *surrender* often connotes giving in to an adversary, or the laying down of arms and acquiescing to the demands of the victor. Some even consider surrender an act of cowardice in which we abandon conviction, purpose, and faith. But surrender can mean much more than that. To surrender to a serious illness means that we cease warring against the illness and acknowledge that it has, in fact, invaded our body. We are not quitting, but making a tactical retreat in order to reassess our position and to reconsider our defenses. We no longer try to avoid the invasion, but instead we calculate our future action in light of the hostile occupation. We find our power in our powerlessness, and our healing through our illness.

*If some aspect of your life is not well, then consider the illness to be the means for an organism to free itself from something foreign to it. In that case you must help it to be ill and to have its whole illness, to let it break out. That is the course of its progress. (Rainer Maria Rilke)*[1]

Usually, when we become ill, we want to know what we should do to get well as soon as possible. This is important, but in our inordinate focus on what we should do (pills, treatments, etc.), we sometimes forget what we should be (compassionate, patient, etc.). Of course we should do whatever we can to recover, but it is also important to befriend the illness. Rather than resisting the reality of our illness like a stiff tree in a hurricane, we allow our self to bend with the wind, and yield to the blow we have sustained.

*Bent, thus preserved whole. (Taoist proverb)*[2]

Serious illness forces us to become more intimate with our self, and offers us an opportunity to connect with our body and appreciate it for the way it has served us for so many years. Facing our illness, we become more aware of our needs and we attempt to meet them. The illness reminds us to make straight the way we live, to stop and rest our weary bones, to allow our creativity to flow, and to refuse to acquiesce to the demands and expectations of the world.

# Remembering Our Holiness

When we remember our inherent holiness (wholeness), it rises up even through the broken pieces of our life. When we remember our holiness, we accept the paradox that to be whole we first embrace our brokenness; to be complete we first acknowledge our incompleteness; and to heal we first enter into our illness. When we remember our holiness we remember our value as human beings in spite of our weaknesses and imperfections, and we accept our self unconditionally. When we remember our holiness we know that we cannot reject parts of our self and remain healthy. Whatever we cut off or deny about our self shows up in mental, physical, and spiritual dysfunction. That which is rejected withers and dies, while that which is embraced lives and thrives. So it is precisely the parts of us that we reject and cast away that we must welcome back into the whole. This includes the parts of us that hold the illness. Only the love of the soul can bring back together that which has been separated. Only the love of the soul can bridge divides, respect differences, accept contradictions, and overcome the forces of judgment and condemnation.

To transcend our illness we must be prepared to face the stark truths about our life. Perhaps there are destructive habitual practices that we need to change. Maybe we are stuck in an unworkable relationship that we should end or a deleterious job that we'd best quit. It may be that we have strayed from our core beliefs and have lost our spiritual way. But when we remember our holiness we identify not with our superficial self that we have invented to defend our self against the world, but with our authentic self that lives in the light of truth. Serious illness compels us to become authentic; it strips away our masks and our pretenses. When we are ill we don't have the energy to put on acts for the sake of looking good or pleasing others. The truth about our self sets us free from the chains of our illness.

When we remember our holiness we become raw and real. This genuineness is a prerequisite for healing. Our authenticity brings congruence between who we are on the inside, including our thoughts and emotions, and who we are on the outside, including our actions and our behavior. When we remember our holiness we find order in the midst of chaos, love in the presence of our enemies, and well-being in spite of our illness.

Healing has the rhythm of the seasons. In its autumn we are left bare and vulnerable; in its winter we lay fallow, restoring our energy, healing our wounds, and gestating the expectant seed of recovery. In its spring we begin to resurrect, and in its summer we burst into new life.

*In the depth of winter I finally learned that there lay within me an invincible summer. (Albert Camus)*[3]

# Accepting Our Pain

We all experience physical pain at some level, at some time; it is an integral part of living and dying. Our pain may come from a small cut or rash that quickly heals, or it may be excruciating pain that results from an injury or a chronic and unrelenting illness. Always, physical pain is accompanied by emotional pain and, conversely, emotional pain may manifest as physical pain. Although we may have no freedom from pain, we do have the freedom to choose how we respond to it.

Although our pain is compelling, it is important to remember that we are not our pain. Pain is just something that is happening to us right now. This does not mean that we should try to ignore the pain or otherwise deny it. Instead, we can face off with it and let it accompany us in our daily living. We can look at it, touch it, breathe into it, accept it, and even befriend it. We can move with it rather than against it, attend to it rather than disregard it, and honor it rather than disparage it.

We have been conditioned to resist pain, so it is very difficult to stop resisting it, not to mention accept it. Yet, this is exactly what we need to do if we are to deal effectively with it. Accepting our pain with gentleness and patience does not mean that we capitulate to it; rather, we acknowledge that it is happening to us, without resisting it. While we want to diminish our pain, our goal is not to eliminate it completely from our life, because we need pain to stay safe and alive. It serves as a warning gauge for us when there is something wrong with our body, mind, or spirit. Without pain we would not know we were having a heart attack or that a bone was broken. Sometimes our physical pain serves to heal that which is nonphysical by forcing us to stop and take notice of how we are living. It may be that our physical pain is telling us what our head has not dared to tell us. When nothing else gets our attention, pain tolls its bell and it will do so until it is heard.

The commonality of pain can serve as a bridge between otherwise different individuals. Pain teaches us to be compassionate toward others in a way that comes only from having felt the pain ourself. We learn that we are not alone in our pain and that sharing the pain with others takes some of the sting out of it. Pain can also teach us to be compassionate toward our self. We can tend to our self in the same manner we would care for others who are in pain. We can respond to our own needs, and we can work to alleviate our own pain in loving ways. Pain teaches us to be interdependent with others, because when we become vulnerable and are in need of help, pain opens us up to receive the love of others as they respond to our painful condition.

Sometimes our pain compels us to seek solace beyond our self and beyond the limitations of others. Sometimes there is nowhere else to turn but within. In prayer and meditation we cry from our pain to receive what we need to get us through the night. When, because of our pain, we can't pray as we want, we can let our pain be our prayer. When, because of our pain, we feel that we have nothing to offer at the altar of love, we can offer up our pain. In prayer and meditation our body and mind slow down and enter a place of calmness and peace. In this environment pain lessens because it meets no resistance. In prayer and meditation we notice our pain in a nonjudgmental way and breathe into it. Loving attention to the pain helps dissipate it.

*When pain is to be borne, a little courage helps more than much knowledge, a little human sympathy more than much courage, and the least tincture of the love of God more than all. (C. S. Lewis)[4]*

Sometimes, when our illness has wracked our body with excruciating pain and we are feeling so nauseous that we would welcome death, we are not concerned about the state of the soul. When our heart is in despair and our mind is clouded and confused, all we care about is getting through the next moment. Nothing matters more to us than to end the agony. In the midst of the pain we feel so powerless that we can't even call upon our spiritual resources for help. My friend Joni says that at times like these the spirit within prays for us. She says, "It is like prayer that comes from the deepest deep ..."

Besides having lost a teenage son to suicide, Joni suffers from several chronic, painful, and disabling illnesses, including Bell's palsy. Some days Joni cannot even get out of bed; other days she is at her computer until the early hours of the morning writing inspirational books. She is honest about the devastating effects of her afflictions; yet, her commitment to serve others through her writing and bereavement ministry is unwavering. Joni is one of my heroes because she epitomizes the transcendence of illness through the power of belief. She does not hesitate to speak of pain and hope in the same breath. In *Tall in Spirit: Meditations for the Chronically Ill*, Joni writes,

The illness that has physically diminished me has also ravaged my inner landscape, changing me as drastically as the woods have been changed by the floodwaters. A transformation has been taking place in my soul, gouging out whole banks where waters once ran deep, overrunning tame places, and flooding my inner terrain. Many of my old and familiar inner parts have been washed out by the raging waters of chronic illness. I don't know precisely at what point I began recognizing this inner wildness. I think I felt it happening long before I understood what it was.

Joni writes on,

There is nothing soft or gentle about long-term illness. Its force has the power to ravage like raging floodwaters, and its bite is like that of a caged animal. It has driven me wild. Sometimes I think it is this wildness that will save me. Sometimes, when the illness is severe, I feel a wildness in me that defies description, like a wolf that has been stuck in a cage and is howling to get out. A tame woman could never howl and this journey requires howling in the most prayerful, ferocious sense.

She adds, "The closest I can come to explaining this is to say that it is like prayer that comes from the deepest deep, wild and passionate for life and freedom."[5]

# Awakening Our Faith

Sometimes serious illness or a close encounter with death can be the catalyst for profound spiritual awakening. How ironic that sometimes an illness can bring about the very faith that we need for deep healing. In the face of illness we may enter into a deeper relationship with our divine essence. It is a relationship that has always been, but our illness forces us to stop and become aware of it. Our illness can be the cause that turns us within in search of that which does not sicken and never dies. It can strengthen our resolve to grow our love and deepen our faith. This manner of faith is not contingent on the circumstances of the day; rather, it is a permanent force by which we live regardless of the condition of our health.

Our faith does not always heal us from our physical infirmities. It offers no guarantee against serious or terminal illness. We all know examples of those whom we have considered spiritually mature and yet have suffered from serious illness or have died from their illness. We also know of those who have refused to entertain the role of spirituality in life and yet have lived long and healthy lives. Sometimes illness and death happen randomly when we least expect with no rhyme or reason.

Our illness makes us afraid, but our faith helps us to face courageously what is. Our illness brings pain, but in faith we cease to struggle against the pain and allow it to temper us. As a result of our illness we lose our independence, but in faith we learn humility and set aside the illusion of self-sufficiency. Our illness kills our dreams and aspirations, but in faith we dream new dreams and set our sights on even higher realms. In illness we lose our way and become confused, but in faith we do our soul work and listen to our inner knowing.

We may pray long and hard for deliverance from our illness without receiving any apparent relief. We may beg, bargain, promise, threaten, and cajole the powers of heaven for a sign that all will be well, but no sign is given. Our belief is not that God will necessarily come to rescue us from our illness; rather, we believe that God is with us even in the abyss of hell, even in the suffering of our illness. We believe that we are given the patience, compassion, and self-love to remain in the reality of what is happening to us physically, mentally, and spiritually, and to create good out of it.

To pray for a specific healing may be presumptuous of us since we are not privy to the whole cosmic picture, but to be prayerful as we confront our illness is another matter. A prayerful heart is open to whatever comes and is hopeful that all things, including illness, can work toward the ultimate good. A prayerful heart accepts illness as a natural part of life. This does not mean that we do not do whatever we can do to avoid getting sick and to heal our self as we can. It means that in prayer and meditation we tap our inner vision that helps us see our illness with the perspective of eternity. When we pray and meditate we enter the sacred space of the soul, where we open to the healing power of love. No longer are we content with the healing of the flesh. In prayer and meditation we set our sights on the healing of our whole self, which is, healing into holiness.

*I learned to pray for my real desire, to fix my attention on the wholeness that I wanted for myself or for someone else, and not to refuse any temporary symptoms that God through nature might use in order to bring about that wholeness. (Agnes Sanford)[6]*

# Evoking Our Power of Belief

Belief is the strong confidence we have in something or someone. It is a force that can override our doubts. It is a truth to which we cling with trust and conviction that prompts us to act or desist from acting. The power of belief was brought home to me rather vividly early in life by the Walt Disney animated movie *Dumbo*. Dumbo did not believe that he could fly and was afraid to try until his mouse friend convinced him that he could as long as he wore a particular feather in his cap. With his belief in the magical power of the feather, Dumbo took off flying. When he accidentally lost his feather, Dumbo also lost his faith in flying and began diving toward the ground. The mouse quickly explained to Dumbo that the real power was not in the feather, but in Dumbo himself. Buoyed by the power of belief in his own ability, Dumbo soared once more into the air.

The power of belief does not change the reality of our illness as much as it changes how we respond to our illness, which, in turn, affects how we heal. Some people believe that if their faith is strong enough, they will never experience illness. They claim that "true believers" do not put their trust in doctors, medicines, or treatments, but rather, deliver themselves into "the hands of God." But if we believe that pharmaceuticals, hospitals, and medical personnel are also the hands of God, then we can also put our faith in them. Actually, our belief does not have to be that the attending physician can heal us, but that she knows which treatments and medications to use that will clear the way for our intrinsic natural healing energy to do its work.

*According to your faith let it be done to you. (Matthew 9:29)*

What do we believe about illness? Do we believe that it is a punishment for our misdeeds or that it comes because we have been lacking in faith? Do we believe that we are being tested or that we are being taught a lesson? Is healing reserved for those who are obedient and acquiescent to a particular religious tradition? Do we believe that illness is something of which to be ashamed or about which to feel guilty? Do we believe that our illness is a manifestation of evil? Or do we believe that illness is a natural part of life and that it is a manifestation of the disharmony or imbalance of our life force?

What we believe about life also impacts our health. If we live believing that the world is a frightening place, we are probably anxious and worried about every little thing. We expect the worst to happen, and we are bound to be generally negative in our outlook on life. This affects our immune system detrimentally and sets us up for illness. If the beliefs we have about our self are narrow and constricted, our physical, mental, and spiritual health will be likewise. If, on the other hand, our beliefs are broad and expansive, healing will probably follow.

We give power over to whatever we fear. In illness we feel great fear because we don't know what to expect. It is said that fear is the opposite of faith, but actually, fear is misplaced faith in that which we fear. Because belief is so powerful, when we believe we will become ill, chances are we will. When we believe that we will heal from our illness, we increase our chances of getting well. In prayer and meditation our fear is overcome with courage. This is not a faith that all will be well, but a faith that, no matter what happens, we have been endowed with what it takes to handle it. What we imagine as real is accepted as real by our unconscious mind and is treated as real by our body.

What we believe about death affects how we live out our life and how we respond to the ups and downs of our health. There is a major difference between our intrinsic survival instinct, which serves to animate our defense mechanism against life-threatening circumstances, and an inordinate fear of death. The former keeps us alive; the latter may make us ill as a result of anxiety and the self-fulfilling prophecy of affliction and morbidity. When we believe that nothing is permanent, we are not surprised or shocked to experience deterioration and decomposition of all that is, including our body and mind. Change is the only constant, and when we are willing to accept that nothing stays the same we can adjust to what is instead of clinging to what was. Our belief in impermanence enhances our ability to heal.

*It is the nature of all things that form to dissolve again. (Buddha)*

Gratitude is a belief that we are blessed. It is an attitude of appreciation of what is and what has been. Recognizing and acknowledging the good, even when it is found among the bad, lifts our spirit and summons life-giving chemicals in our body to move us toward healing. A grateful heart is usually a peaceful heart, and peacefulness produces an excellent environment for healing. Healing begins in the soul. The soul seeks harmony, promotes peace, welcomes joy, and offers kindness; it is a divine instrument of healing and the abode of holiness.

# Obeying Natural Law

Sometimes we are tempted to defy natural law, to ignore logic, and to counteract our instinct for survival, all in the name of "faith." Yet, this is not faith, but folly. Well-being is about choice. When we deliberately put ourselves at risk of becoming ill or being hurt, there is a strong possibility that we will be, regardless of what we believe. We may be able through mind control to walk on hot coals without getting burned, but no amount of mind control will protect us from full exposure to the AIDS virus or from skydiving without a parachute. We cannot jump off a cliff in defiance of the law of gravity based on the belief that angels will deliver us from all harm. Our belief that heavenly forces will protect us should not promote stupidity or fanaticism. Belief does not require that we suspend our intelligence. Faith is not a synonym for irresponsibility. In fact, it is our faith in the ways of nature that makes us responsible caretakers of our own welfare. Wisdom dictates that maladies can be cured, not in spite of natural law, but rather, in harmony with it.

Even when we do not consciously choose illness, we sometimes choose behaviors that may contribute to illness. When, on the other hand, we are conscious of the laws of nature and obey them, we are more apt to live in ways that promote and sustain good health. The word *obey* means "to listen" and "to hear." So when we listen to and obey the laws of creation, we are respecting the divine design.

*For it was you who formed my inward parts; you knit me together in my mother's womb. I praise you, for I am fearfully and wonderfully made. Wonderful are your works; that I know very well. (Psalm 139:13–14)*

We are not responsible for all the illness that is visited upon us, but we are responsible for minimizing the odds of becoming ill. We are responsible for the choices we make regarding our welfare. To love our self as we love others is to opt for those actions and abstentions that enhance our well-being. We can choose to give our self only those things that are healthy for our mind, body, and spirit. We can choose not to work in excess, and to exercise appropriately for our age and circumstances. We can play periodically and rest often, and we can remember to tend to the soul through prayer and meditation. An illness can be temporarily relieved, but for healing we need to obey the laws of nature and address the root of our illness, be it physical, emotional, or spiritual.

To believe in natural law is to believe in our inherent capacity to heal—that is, the natural inclination of our being to move toward homeostasis. At a level beyond our awareness, our body is working without ceasing to protect us from illness. Cells, organs, and blood are dedicated to keeping us safe from harm. But our trust in our natural ability to stay healthy does not exonerate us from the responsibility to take good care of our self and to avoid harm or illness whenever possible.

*Trust in God and tie your camel to a post. (A Sufi saying)*

Natural law stipulates that stagnation leads to disease, while profluence promotes healing. Like the stagnant water of an obstructed stream that putrefies and hosts pestilence and disease, our life force can also be blocked, resulting in disease and the dysfunction of our body, mind, and spirit. And just as the stream flows again when the dam is broken through, we are more likely to heal when the flow of our vital energy is restored. Without movement and transformation we may wither and die; with fluency we can heal and thrive. As the stream flows back to the ocean, our being flows back to wholeness.

To love and be loved is the greatest medicine of all. I remember a time when my sister Alicia was terribly depressed. She went to several doctors, including a psychiatrist, to shake this terrible mental illness, but nothing seemed to work, not even the medications that were prescribed. Her depression continued for some time with no relief. Finally, Alicia connected with a therapist who was able to help her. I asked my sister some time after her depression had lifted what had made the difference in her treatment. I wanted to know why so many mental health professionals had been unable to help her and then suddenly there was one who was able to bring her out of her depression. Was it perhaps a more effective medication that she had been prescribed? Was it a new alternative treatment that she had received? What had helped her to heal? Alicia knew exactly what had happened. She said it all had to do with her therapist. "She showed me kindness," she said. She added that the empathy and compassion that the therapist had offered her provided the caring environment and the encouragement that she needed to evoke her own healing forces.

*Pleasant words are like honeycomb, sweetness to the soul and health to the body. (Proverbs 16:24)*

# Trusting Our Healers

Through years of therapy Sharon came to believe in her ability to heal from the effects of the traumatic and inhumane treatment she had experienced in childhood. Her belief in those who helped her and in the power of forgiveness and self-love gave her a peace she had never known before.

I met Sharon toward the beginning of my counseling and psychotherapy practice. At first I treated her for depression and family problems. It wasn't until much later that she was also diagnosed with dissociative identity disorder, what we used to call multiple personality disorder. As a child Sharon had suffered severe physical, sexual, and psychological abuse at the hands of satanic cult members, which included her parents. The nature of the abuse was unimaginable. The only way Sharon was able to survive such trauma was to mentally leave her body through dissociation and create different personalities within herself to take the abuse for her. The various personalities stayed conscious in order to deal with the abuse, but Sharon became amnesic. Her ability to dissociate saved her sanity and perhaps her life.

The psyche of a child cannot contain or sustain that much trauma, so it either collapses into some kind of psychosis or it dissociates. Dissociation is nature's way of coping with overwhelming trauma. Amnesia protects the child from having to deal with her traumatic experiences directly until she is ready to face them later in life. The amnesia usually begins to wear thin around midlife, and glimpses of the traumatic memories begin to surface and interfere with everyday life.

Sometimes it's the death of the perpetrators that triggers the return of memories.

Sharon was able to dissociate often throughout her horrendous childhood, thus creating dozens of personalities. It took several years of therapy for the personalities to begin to trust me enough to reveal themselves to me. Each personality had a specific job to do to help Sharon cope with the trauma that was happening to her. One would be the holder of the physical pain, another would guard the emotions from getting out of control, another would do the rational thinking for the group of personalities, while yet another would be the "protector." One served as a mother for the infant preverbal personalities, and one was "the spiritual one." There was even a personality who was designated as "the student." She was the one responsible for attending school and acting "normal" as though nothing out of the ordinary was happening at home.

The roles of the personalities were so real in Sharon's mind that they played out physiologically. Sharon had diabetes, wore glasses to read, and suffered from fibromyalgia and chronic fatigue syndrome. Incredibly, however, one of the personalities was free of diabetic symptoms, another could actually read without glasses, and yet another had no signs of either fibromyalgia or chronic fatigue. Each personality looked different from the others. When the personalities visited me, Sharon's facial muscles were held differently for each, mannerisms changed, her voice was altered, and handwriting was markedly different among the personalities who could write. The preverbal personalities, of course, could not communicate with me at all, but they did show up.

When we first started working with the various personalities, Sharon hated them because they made her feel as if she were crazy. The truth is, dissociative identity disorder is not a psychosis but an ingenious adaptation made by the psyche in an attempt to preserve sanity. It works under the same principle as the palm tree bending with the windstorm in order not to break. As therapy went forward Sharon was able to befriend and appreciate the personalities for all their help.

The personalities were, of course, a figment of Sharon's imagination, but this is what is so amazing about the propensity of the psyche to seek homeostasis. Because Sharon was able to split into different personalities, she was able to give order to chaos, and to bear what no child should ever have to experience. It was a strategy for survival and it worked, but not without dire consequences. As an adult, Sharon functioned well for many years as a wife, mother, and registered nurse. She was a very intelligent and high-functioning woman. At a certain age, however, the memories that had been held safely by the personalities began to seep into her daily life. She became severely depressed and anxious and did not know why. The amnesia was wearing off, and the reality of what had happened to her was breaking into her consciousness. Her life was becoming unraveled, and she was forced to seek help.

It is difficult for any of us to trust others enough to accept their help; it is next to impossible for those who have been severely abused to trust others, even health professionals. Yet, over the years Sharon learned to accept help from others as she healed herself. She understood that sometimes a partnership for healing can be formed between the ill person and the health professional. She wrote in her journal,

There are those in our lives who bless us with their presence. They stand as close as possible to the flames to be near us. It matters not to them that they may get singed and sooty. They have the courage to face our conflagration and not avert their eyes from the pain and suffering of another. They have the life-affirming virtue of honesty. Instead of offering some meaningless platitude like, "It doesn't look that bad," they affirm the awfulness we see within as the truth of our lives. They love enough to tend the fires so they don't burn out of control. They love enough to push and poke the embers around to help balance the purging so that in the end we are not destroyed or left untouched by the holy flames, rather, that the necessary purging will be as complete as possible. They add more fuel when necessary by their gifts of encouragement and support, and their respect and belief that we will not be consumed by the flames, but rather, transformed.[7]

During her therapy Sharon struggled with the myriad emotions that plagued her heart. She wrote,

Admitting my feelings, bringing them out into the light of day felt like ripping my skin from my flesh. I felt raw, naked, drained, guilty, embarrassed, and humiliated. For so long these feelings had been a part of me, and now they lay there exposed, visible in all their ugliness and repulsiveness, but at last apart, separate from me.[8]

Sharon was aware of all she had lost as a consequence of her traumatic childhood. She was also aware of the necessity for grieving those losses. She wrote,

We must acknowledge, honor, embrace, and grieve those dramatic losses, especially the intangibles: loss of childhood, loss of innocence, loss of trust, loss of self-esteem, loss of self-confidence, loss of the ability to form healthy relationships, loss of the ability to be intimate with others, loss of a lifetime of participating in life, loss of potential, loss of our sense of holiness, loss of security, loss of peace, loss of love.[9]

Sharon wrote of healing through forgiveness:

As time passed, I knew with more and more certainty that I did indeed have to forgive those people in my life who had hurt me so. I needed to do it not so much for their sakes, but for mine, for me to grow, to come closer to that to which I am called. How could I forgive someone for a lifetime of pain and bitterness? My head wanted to but my heart continued to refuse.[10]

She continued in her journal,

One day I drove out to a secluded area near my home and found myself alone with God. I finally was able to say the words, "I forgive," but the act of forgiving them had to come from God. By myself I was unable to accomplish this. Only by asking God to help me, to accept my desire to forgive, along with my inability to do it, to forgive through me and for me, was true forgiveness brought into being.[11]

*Psyche* means "soul," and Sharon's psychotherapy was indeed soul work. Her life was spiritually based, so her psychological therapy was permeated with spiritual work. Toward the end of her therapy Sharon's personalities began to integrate spontaneously, but Sharon's integration was more than psychological. Though Sharon's depression lifted, she continued to suffer from other physical maladies. In spite of her physical illnesses, Sharon's profound faith had made her whole. She died of heart failure years later, but not before she had experienced healing into holiness.

# Healing Our Self

I f we were to observe a wound on our body heal at an accelerated pace, we would notice that the healing takes place from the inside out. This is how all healing happens, in us and through us. There is within us an impelling life force that drives us toward homeostasis and equanimity. But healing our self is not just a matter of pushing against what ails us, obliterating it with the force of will, or overpowering it with a pharmaceutical assault. It bears repeating that it involves befriending our illness, getting to know it, and learning more from it. Healing requires us to enter into the full experience of the illness with our heart and mind wide open.

When we get sick our initial focus is usually on what may be hurting our body. Our first question is, "What do I have (as in heart failure or cancer)?" Yet, the question we should also be asking is, "What am I missing (as in peace, contentment, or spiritual connection)?" When we understand the needs of our body, mind, and spirit, we are better able to meet those needs and begin healing into holiness. Of course we take prescribed medications and employ medical treatments and procedures when it is appropriate to do so, but awareness of what has been missing for us can guide our response to our illness.

One thing that may be missing for us is the desire to heal. That might sound ridiculous when we assume that we all want to be healthy, but sometimes our unconscious has a mind of its own. The body takes its orders from the unconscious desire of the mind. Desire for wellness makes all the difference in the world. Conversely, if we believe unconsciously that healing from serious illness will work to our disadvantage, we will probably sabotage any attempt to heal us. For example, if getting well means that our monthly disability checks on which we depend will stop or the attention we receive for being sick will stop or that we will have to return to a job that we hate, then we receive a "secondary gain" by staying sick. In such cases we don't have a sincere desire to get well and we probably won't.

Another thing that may be missing for us when we are ill is the belief that we can be healed. If, for example, we don't believe in the intrinsic capability of our body to heal or if we have no faith in the doctor who is attending us or the medicine he is prescribing, our chances of healing are diminished. Healing is not initiated from without, but from within the person who is ill.

We may be missing necessary grief. Unresolved grief can block our life force and lead to illness. Life is full of losses, and each loss needs to be acknowledged and grieved. But we may be afraid to feel the devastating pain of loss and may be shutting our self down emotionally in order not to feel it. Consequently, we shut down all feelings, including joy, and we may become depressed and physically ill. The dark cloud will not lift until we are willing to consciously enter into the pain that comes with loss. The wound is the door through which we enter into healing and holiness.

We may be missing the experience and expression of our emotions. When we block our emotions we disconnect from our self, and this disconnection may lead to illness. We may be afraid to feel our emotions lest they get out of hand and we lose control. When we suppress our anger, hurt, sadness, or any emotion that we consider negative, we deny our self a natural means of expressing externally what is happening internally. There is nothing detrimental about any of our emotions; the problem is how we react to them. Not dealing with our anger, for example, may affect our immune system over time. Our feelings can serve as a reliable early warning system that alerts us to what is good for us and what is not. Of course, a safe environment is essential for us if we are to risk exposure of our feelings. Whether it is a friend, a therapist, or a spiritual guide who listens to us or a journal in which we write, we are truly blessed if we have been granted a secure repository.

We may be missing self-love. We may be taking care of everyone except our self, and tending to the needs of others at our expense. Of course we want to be kind and generous to others, but it is crucial that we include our self in the equation. Some of us confuse generosity with doing for others so they will love us. They are not the same thing. We cannot buy love with our service. When we keep putting out our energy for others and neglect our self in the process, we set our self up to get overwhelmed, exhausted, and sick. When we are putting out so much more than we are taking in, we need to invert the golden rule and "do for our self what we would do for others"; that is, be kind, considerate, thoughtful, and solicitous toward our self. We can be conscious of the stress that ordinary life imposes on us and go out of our way to calm and soothe our self through meditation, music, and time for our self.

Self-love includes ridding our self of that which is toxic. Healing comes through the purgation of anything or anyone that is toxic to our mind, body, or spirit. Even toxic beliefs can make us ill. Negative beliefs about our self or others can block natural mental development. They can influence our outlook on life and hence our behavior. It may be toxic substances to which we have become addicted that keep us sick. These are the hardest to purge because we use them to assuage the pain that comes with living. We believe they bring us comfort, or at least mitigate our agitation and anxiety but, of course, substance abuse provides only temporary relief and leaves us worse off than before.

We may be missing the opportunity to be creative. Every one of us is creative in one way or another. Our creativity can produce a grand composition, a classical novel, or a sculpture that lasts through the ages. It can also be a special meal that we fix for our family, a quilt we make for a loved one, or a garden we plant and nurture. What we create is not as important as the life force that flows through us to create it. But when the flow of our creativity is blocked, we may become ill. It is like a clogged artery that cannot carry the lifeblood to the heart. It is only when we remove the blockage—whether it be physical, psychological, or spiritual—that the creative forces can begin to restore our health.

We may be missing patience. When it comes to healing, we are impatient. We want wellness and we want it right now. Impatience brings stress to our body and agitates our mind. Such impatience overlooks the wisdom inherent in the natural healing process. Even when it appears to us that we are still sick, healing is already taking place in its own way and in its own time. Patience is our belief that good will come by waiting. Such patience serves us well as we confront our illnesses, diseases, and injuries. When we believe in the healing process, we can wait trustingly. This may mean that we give medication time to take effect, that we allow sufficient time for bones to mend, and that, as patients, we allow others to tend to us according to their abilities and their schedules.

We may be missing reconciliation with our self. If we have been broken in days gone by, it is only by remembering what happened to us and dealing with it emotionally and spiritually that we can begin to heal. Remembering means that we put the pieces of our life back together with some sense of continuity. If we can understand what happened to us, all the better, but sometimes we have to settle for just getting the story straight.

We may be missing assertiveness. My friend Dorothy was assertiveness personified. Her whole life was a long battle against the devastating effects of polio. This is an acute infectious disease of motor nerves of the spinal cord and brain stem that results in muscular atrophy and skeletal deformity. Confined to a wheelchair from early childhood, Dorothy was forced in the beginning to be dependent on those around her. But because she was left alone in the basement of the house for hours at a time, she learned that, ultimately, she had to fend for herself. It was during those long and lonely hours that Dorothy formed her beliefs about life. She decided that despite her physical limitations, she would be relevant in the world. She finished her education and became a teacher, a profession she dearly loved. She had to fight hard to get her teaching job because in those days there was still strong employment discrimination against the disabled. It was not easy conducting class from a wheelchair, but that was the reality with which Dorothy had to deal. She bought a home and lived alone most of her life. She was married briefly, but her husband died. In a van with modified pedals, she drove herself everywhere until she could no longer drive. Eventually, her disease also forced her to give up teaching.

Dorothy did not attend church regularly, but she was a woman with strong beliefs. She didn't talk about religion much nor did she put much stock in doctrine or dogma. Her faith was her daily living. When she could no longer move her hands, she used a voice-activated computer to write her thoughts. She loved people and people loved her. One year she decided to throw herself a birthday party and invited her special friends. It was fun because Dorothy was fun.

Dorothy's belief was not so much in the possibility of being cured of her disease or of living longer, but in life itself, and in the gift of each moment. She believed in loving-kindness and its impact on the world, one person at a time. She believed that no matter how long she lived or in what condition, she would make the best of it and squeeze the juice out of every day. Post-polio syndrome set in, and doctors gave Dorothy only five years to live. She listened to the prognosis, rejected it, and then took matters into her own hands. I was with Dorothy when she died, not five, but twenty years later.

# Giving Purpose to Our Illness

llness is not the end of our journey; life still waits for our response. There is a force within each one of us that emanates from the essence of the soul. This energy, this motivation, is empowered by a personal reason for living. It is a potent intentionality that gives purpose to our existence, including our illness.

While illness does not come with a predetermined purpose, once it has come, we have the freedom to give it a purpose. When we give our illness a purpose, we are more willing to make a sacrifice of it. To *sacrifice* means to make sacred, to devote or dedicate to a purpose, and to regard with reverence. In other words, to give purpose to our illness is to give it a "why." Our affliction can become purposeful, productive, and even beneficial if it has a reason to be. To sacrifice is to give up something good for something greater. For example, we may choose to consider a heart attack as a blessing because it can force us to slow down, stop smoking, reduce our workload, increase our exercise, and live. The trade-off is a heart attack for a life. Our illness can move us to be more compassionate toward those who are ill and in need of help. Through our illness we can learn patience and tolerance for others. It can teach us to respond to life less frantically and more serenely, and it can remind us of the preciousness of life and the value of every moment.

Giving purpose to our illness may sound grandiose and global, but purpose need not necessarily apply beyond our immediate circle of life. Once I befriended a young woman named Alejandra. I got to know her well at several spiritual retreats we had both attended. She was a peaceful person with a beautiful smile. A single mother of two small children, she had not had an easy time of it. In fact, she had experienced much emotional and physical pain in her twenty-four years of life. It was hard to tell from her demeanor that she was dying of bone cancer. Only her amputated leg and bulging tumors gave it away. Her husband had left her, and her illness limited the time she could spend with her two small children. Her world was coming to an end, yet there was such peace in her face, a peace I did not understand. I visited her over a period of months, including her last days in a hospice setting. I wanted to be supportive of her in every way I could.

One day, not long before Alejandra died, I began asking her probing questions about her philosophy of life and death. I asked her what things she would want to tell the world if she could. I even asked her what she would do with her life if she were granted health and more time to live. As to the profound message she would issue from her deathbed, she had none. She said, however, that she wanted to write a few words to her son and daughter. She had already written a poem of love to her mother. I began to see that Alejandra's scope of life was in the here and now. Her attention was on the immediate, the local, and the real.

To my question about a second go at life, Alejandra said she would not change much if she were to get well and stay alive. She had no plans greater than to go to the park with her children and watch them at play. She said she would want to work and to go for a ride once in a while. She wanted to do "the ordinary things of life" and to live one moment at a time, enjoying it fully, just being. She spoke of simple things, of the present time, and of littleness. She seemed to be saying, "I will just smell this flower one more time before I go."

Alejandra's body was overcome by the cancer and she died soon thereafter, yet she was one of the healthiest persons I have ever known. Her salubrity ran deeper than her killer tumors, and her love transcended illusions of time and space. She was grateful as she looked back on her shortened life and courageous as she faced death prematurely.

Alejandra was buried in a potter's field as anonymously as she had lived. But I had known her, and I will remember her always. A few days before her death she recited for me a few words from her favorite poem: "Life, how much I owe you; Life, I am at peace."

Each person's experience with illness is unique, but there are some commonalities among seriously ill and injured people with which we can all relate. In fact, there seems to be a special connection among those who have been seriously ill or injured. It is a sodality to which we may prefer not to belong, but have nevertheless been inducted into through a severe initiation. There is a compassion shared by those of us who have been seriously ill or injured that transcends all the differences between us. Consider the example of the thousands of combat troops who return from war with traumatic brain injuries, post-traumatic stress disorder, amputation, and burned and mangled bodies. These men and women come from different regions of the country, live different lifestyles, and believe in different religious traditions, yet they share a tragic common denominator: an illness or injury that has altered their lives forever. Returning warriors are as varied as the birds of the sky, yet their afflictions make them of one feather.

*Those who have learned by experience what physical pain and bodily anguish mean belong together all the world over; they are united by a secret bond. (Albert Schweitzer)[12]*

We who have suffered from illness or injury are united by that bond. Another thing we have in common is our freedom to give purpose to our illness or injury. That purpose may be to serve others in spite of our wounds. We can empathize with the ill and injured, and we remember well what helped us in the midst of our anguish. We know who encouraged us and who gave us succor, and we know who lifted us and who brought us peace. It might have been a poem someone read to us in the middle of a sleepless night; it might have been the kind gesture of a caregiver, or a borrowed book that accompanied us through chemotherapy or dialysis. Because we received, we can now give.

There are myriad opportunities for us to use our experience with illness or injury to help others. Much depends on our physical and mental condition, but our skills and talents also play a part. We respond from where we are. We don't have to wait until we have recovered from our illness or injury completely in order to feel compassion for, and connection with, those who suffer as we have. Even if we are still bedridden at home, in a hospital, or in a care facility, we can still be generative with our life. Our help can come in the form of care giving, through a support group, or through a one-on-one listening presence.

Whatever we offer can make a difference in the lives of those who are ill or injured. Our help is more effective when those whom we help know that we understand the nature of their plight because we've been through it our self. In other words, those who have experienced a serious illness or injury are moved to great compassion for others who also suffer.

*If a person has gone through a crisis, died to an old personality, and fought his or her way back to health and a more conscious life, that person may gain a certain quality that enables him or her to put others in touch with theirs as well. (John Sanford)[13]*

My friend Sister Ave is a survivor of sexual assault and now suffers from post-traumatic stress disorder (PTSD). More recently, she was hit by a train that suddenly derailed and crashed into her car. But even as she struggles with her PTSD and heals from her broken bones, Sister Ave continues her spiritual retreat work among the people of the Diocese of Brooklyn. She has offered seminars for men and women who have been victims of sexual abuse and assault, and she wrote a book to help survivors like herself. In her book, *Lights in the Darkness: For Survivors and Healers of Sexual Abuse,* Sister Ave wrote,

Survivors who step forward to help others who have been abused become "Pilgrims of Grace," immersing themselves in the journey of healing life's deepest wounds, discovering new paths, creating new roots, making new friends, and finding new ways to celebrate life. It is truly a gift of grace to lift up one's deeply wounded spirit and bind up one's own brokenness so that another survivor can see some light in the darkness.[14]

On September 11, 2001, that infamous day when terrorists attacked our country, my friend Melanie was experiencing her own personal catastrophe. She had been diagnosed days earlier with breast cancer and on that day was undergoing a mastectomy. Melanie has been a nurse, a university professor, and a massage therapist. Her whole life has been devoted to helping others heal and stay healthy. After the surgery Melanie experienced profound loss on many levels, not the least of which was the strength and energy to continue her massage therapy work. She had helped many men and women heal physically and had many clients depending on her.

We can use our experience with illness as a source of inspiration for our creativity. Depending on our talent, we may choose to express ourselves through art, music, writing, or other creative endeavors. What we create can help others on their journey toward healing. Although Melanie was able to continue singing in the church choir, an activity that was truly life-giving for her, her creative energy was busting at the seams of her heart. She needed to do something constructive with her grief and she still wanted to serve others, so she began to write. At first, Melanie's essays had to do with her cancer, her surgery, and her subsequent chemotherapy treatment and recovery. Later, she started writing about the spiritual response to illness and other adversities of life. In an unpublished essay on Psalm 51, Melanie wrote,

It has always been that when I feel desperately broken, my dependence on God is revealed or, should I say, exposed. It signals to me that I need to turn and listen for the voice of God in my life again. In times when I feel shattered, I experience the presence of God breaking open my stubbornly resistant heart.

Melanie became certified as a spiritual director and has been helping others to heal spiritually. Her gratitude for life and her compassion for those who suffer physically, mentally, or spiritually have fueled her life's work.

While our illness or injury was not caused so that good would come of it, good can indeed come of it. In the wake of our illness, we are now more conscious and more compassionate; we choose to live with greater purpose and intentionality. We move through our experience with illness to touch the lives of others in profoundly healing ways.

# In the Wake of My Illness

ere, I put words to the journey of illness:

*I am sick unto death. I have been scattered across the rocky plains of life, lost to myself and to the world. My options are few, my needs are immediate, and I am awakened by the reality of what is. I can go no further; I must stop now. Illness has laid me low. My will is to continue, to keep on moving; there is so much more to do. Yet, I am powerless now; I am forced into repose. Here, in silence and stillness, my soul begins to heal. From the depths of despair and the agony of illness, the pieces of my life are gathered.*

My will gives way to heaven's call; I follow the ways that lead to hallowed ground. The illness that has brought me down now lifts me to a higher place. I pass through this place of risk and vulnerability, but I do not stay. Courage carries me forth and faith sustains me. I am not alone. I believe in the justice of nature and the compassion of life. My weakness is my strength, and my illness is the genesis of my healing.

In the midst of my infirmity the blessings come. My mind opens so that I might learn the lessons of my illness. My heart expands to receive the love that is born of my surrender. My flesh acquiesces to the demands of my condition. From this infernal infirmity the Phoenix rises, not in spite of the flames, but because of them. From my head to my feet I am sanctified. My bones may be broken and my blood spilled, yet my core is pure and my soul is whole.

# If Our Illness Becomes Terminal

I f our illness has been diagnosed as terminal, physical healing is no longer an option, but healing into holiness always is. Even in the light of death, it is inherent in our humanity to strive in faith toward holiness. Facing the inevitability of our death prompts us to integrate into our daily life the reality of our transiency in this world, and we develop an even greater appreciation for life.

Impending death enlivens us, and our senses become especially keen. Everything we see, hear, taste, or touch is marvelous to us. Suddenly we are in awe of the unremarkable sparrow searching for breakfast in our backyard, and the homely bush that we took for granted now becomes for us the epitome of life. We hear the sound of children's laughter and our heart smiles; the smell of the desert after rain and the fragrance of the creosote refresh our soul. Nothing feels as wild as a handful of thick dog fur, and nothing is as soft as the petal of a flower. As far as we know, we may be experiencing what is before us for the last time. It is sobering to realize that what we have taken for granted could be lost to us in a heartbeat. It seems that which is limited is cherished more than that which is limitless, and life is savored all the more because it is fleeting.

Our awareness that we will soon die is not the same as constantly obsessing about our mortality; rather, it is staying mindful of its reality. When we stop to think that our life is going to end, perhaps sooner than we anticipate, the passing moment takes on great significance. Now is all we can really count on. Now is when we can pray, love, and create. Now is when we can reach for the stars, fulfilling our dreams; howl at the moon, expressing our emotions; and follow the sun, giving flight to our adventurous spirit.

When we realize that any day could be our last, we start asking questions of our self. What if today is my last day to live? Is what I am doing really necessary for me to do? Is it necessary for me to say what I am about to say? What does it matter what others say about me as long as I am being true to myself and to God? Is the matter before me as important as I am making it? How do I want to spend today? Am I being congruent with what I believe? What does love prompt me to do?

We prepare to die by putting our affairs in order and saying our good-byes, but also by breaking bread at the banquet of life and tasting the sweet wine of love. We prepare to die by remembering who we have been and what we have done, but also by forgiving our self for our iniquities and absolving others of their trespasses against us.

In anticipation of imminent death, we withdraw to our personal garden to prepare for that which is to come. Our heart is heavy with fear and sorrow. We are alone even if others are with us; we have no defenses, no defenders, and no escape. The experience of dying comes like a hurricane that strips the landscape to its barest state. Whatever it is that we have clung to in life is torn from us as death approaches. All of our facades are ripped away, and our pretenses vanish. We are left naked to the bone with no robes to cover our humanness and no lies to cover our shame.

What is right before us, what is happening in the passing moment, is what is important now. Our focus is on the immediate realities: alleviating our pain, a bird singing outside the window, a visit from a friend. We have less on which to focus because impending death gives us fewer choices. As our world contracts, our faith expands. The past disappears from our mind, and we know there is no future. Our commitment is to the eternal now.

There is a point at the threshold of death when we accept and adapt to the conditions in which we find our self, including physical pain, uncertainty, and loss of functionality. We begin to empty our self of everything except the love we've given and the love we've received, for it is love alone that transcends the dimensions of our being.

We love life but we do not cling to it; rather, because we revere life, we are open and ready to experience death as the next phase of life. Death, after all, is not termination, but the ultimate healing. Death is like a swiftly flowing river that will not be halted or suppressed. Try as we may to interfere with it, it keeps flowing resolutely toward the sea from whence it came. We cannot stop the river, but we can flow with it graciously and gratefully, believing that

> ... *life and death are one, even as the river and the sea are one* ... *(Khalil Gibran)*[15]

# Afterword

---

The Twenty-Third Psalm (paraphrased):

*God tends to me in my brokenness; my every need is met. God invites me to stop and rest my body, still my mind, and recover my soul. God exhorts me to change my ways in the name of wholeness.*

*In the midst of the dark night of my affliction, I am graced with the courage to overcome even the worst malignity. Your dominion over my life strengthens me. Your nourishment abounds alongside my infirmities; you sanctify my ailing flesh with your healing balm; my spirit rejoices.*

*My well-being will be sustained by benevolence and forgiveness, and the presence of God will never leave me.*

# Endnotes

1. Rainer Maria Rilke, *Letters to a Young Poet* (San Rafael, California: The Classic Wisdom Collection, New World Library, 1992), 86.
2. Ellen M. Chen, *Tao Te Ching: A New Translation with Commentary* (New York: Paragon House, 1989), 124.
3. Albert Camus, brainyquote.com/quotes/authors/a/albert_camus_2.html
4. C. S. Lewis, *The Problem of Pain* (New York: HarperCollins, 1940).
5. Joni Woelfel, *Tall in Spirit* (Chicago: Acta Publications, 1999), 66.
6. Agnes Sanford, *Sealed Orders* (Alachua, Florida: Bridge-Logos, 1972).
7. Adolfo Quezada, *Heart Songs: Yearnings of a Wounded Soul (unpublished)).*
8. Quezada, Heart Songs
9. Quezada, Heart Songs
10. Quezada, Heart Songs
11. Quezada, Heart Songs
12. Albert Schweitzer, as quoted in *Close to the Bone: Life-Threatening Illnesses and the Search for Meaning* by Jean Shinoda Bolen, M.D. (New York: Scribner, 1996), 182.
13. John A. Sanford, *Healing and Wholeness* (New York: Paulist Press, 1997), 81.
14. Ave Clark, O.P., *Lights in the Darkness: For Survivors and Healers of Sexual Abuse* (New York: Resurrection Press, 1993), 100.
15. Khalil Gibran, brainyquote.com/quotes/authors/k/khalil_gibran.html